The Gift

Written by Robert F. Morneau

Illustrated by Marjorie M. Mau

 PAULIST PRESS ● New York ● Mahwah, N.J.

Published by:
Paulist Press, 997 Macarthur Blvd., Mahwah, New Jersey 07430
www.paulistpress.com

Printed and bound in the United States of America.

Designed by Christine LaCount

Cataloging-in-Publication Data
Morneau, Robert F. The Gift/story by Robert F. Morneau;
illustrated by Marjorie M. Mau.
Summary: Through his close relationship with a pumpkin, a rabbit learns
about his environment and how sacrifice can lead to new life.
1. Pumpkins—Juvenile Fiction 2. Rabbits—Juvenile Fiction
3. Friendship—Juvenile Fiction
[1. Friendship—Fiction 2. Life cycles—Fiction]
I. Mau, Marjorie M., ill. II. title 1995 [E]
Library of Congress Catalog Card Number 94-78138
ISBN 0-8091-6673-9

With gratitude for their support and assistance, we, author and illustrator, dedicate this book to our families:

• • •

Jim, Margaret, Sarah, Joseph, Mary Frances, Emmett, Rudy, Pip, Ann, Sue, Kay, Joan, Mother and Father

Robert

• • •

David, Michael, Christine, Susan, Daniel, Christopher, Buddy, my Mother and the memory of my Father

Marjorie

• • •

and to our friend and literary agent:
Sister Mary Samuel Brunner, O.S.F.

*O*nce upon a summer, when the wind was friendly, the rain was kind, and the sun was wonderfully warm, Farmer Jim planted eleven hills of pumpkins.

Farmer Jim had a fancy for pumpkins. Maybe it was his cravings for pumpkin pie. Or maybe it was because his children feared the dark and they believed lanterns made of giant pumpkins drove away the goblins of the night.

Probably it was Farmer Jim's love of the beauty of pumpkins dotting the hills that made his heart dance with joy.

One day Sammy, the king rabbit on the farm, cut through the pumpkin patch on his way to visit some tasty carrots.

In the patch lived Angela, Sammy's very good friend and the loveliest pumpkin in Farmer Jim's patch.

In fact, Sammy was secretly
in love with Angela.

Their romance began early one morning when
rabbits dance on the dew and pumpkins are
warmed in the first rays of dawn.

Sammy liked Angela's round smile. Angela loved
Sammy's lovely, listening ears.

Some days they talked for hours about the clouds,
politics, flies, and even religion.

Sammy told Angela what he could. He told her that he had
forty-two sisters and brothers, that his favorite briar patch was
down by the creek, and that carrot juice made his nose wiggle.
But Sammy was unable to express his deepest thoughts.

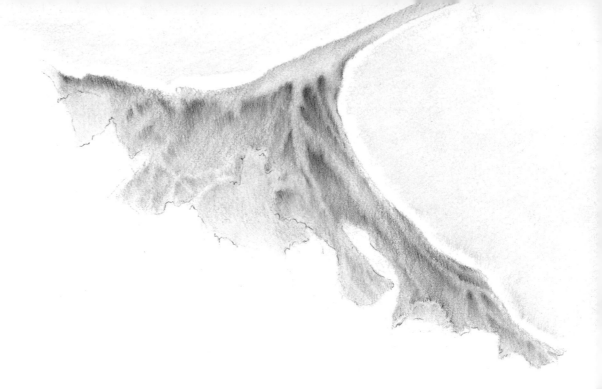

Angela was a very special pumpkin. She somehow, somewhere learned to tell what went on deep inside her. She found words to wrap around her most inner thoughts and feelings.

"Sammy," Angela said, "I've never told any pumpkin nor any rabbit what I am going to tell you. And when the snows begin to fall and the geese have all gone south and you are cold with loneliness please remember my story."

Sammy nodded.

"One morning, when I was small and green and rather ugly, I felt a surge like a lump in the throat, a leap in the heart, or a shiver down the spine. I knew I was growing and changing. Then I noticed I wasn't alone. A strong vine held me tight. I began that day to call him Mr. V. Soon he began to whisper secrets to me, especially when the stars came out and the garden had quieted down after a hard day of growing."

Sammy's ears stood straight up so he wouldn't miss a word.

"Mr. V's secrets were amazing! He told me that all the juices that he gave me to make me wonderfully round, wonderfully orange, and wonderfully beautiful came from the soil. He calls the soil Mrs. S. He said Mrs. S is a generous soul who loves the carrots and corn, the rutabagas and squash, and even the unfriendly zucchini.

"Now, Mr. V and Mrs. S work together and work hard because so many people come to the garden with empty stomachs. Knowing this I say thanks about three hundred times a day and I hope that Mrs. S and Mr. V can hear me."

"I believe they can," Sammy said.

"Another very good friend of mine is the Day Star.
I think you call her the sun. Without Ms. DS there
would be no light, no warmth, nothing
but darkness and coldness. Ms. DS
is so faithful, every day she helps
me grow."

There was more to Angela's story, but before she could finish telling Sammy about Ms. DS thick black clouds quickly blocked Sammy and Angela's view of her.

"Ms. Rain," Angela laughed, "what fun it is to feel all the splashes and watch the puddles forming!"

"Ms. R comes down often, sometimes like cats and dogs, and takes away my thirst," Angela explained, "and when I get in fights or squabbles with other pumpkins Ms. R comes to clean off the mud that we throw at each other and that puts us back on good terms."

Sammy's face twitched as the raindrops hit his brow. "Oh Sammy," Angela said, "you're getting wet and your ears are drooping."

Sammy ran for cover in Farmer Jim's barn and shook his fur dry. While he stared at the falling rain he noticed Farmer Jim standing next to him. Farmer Jim nodded to Sammy and Sammy wiggled his nose back. There they both watched the rain in silence.

Sammy thought about Mr. V and Mrs. S, Ms. R and Ms. DS. He had never realized that Angela had so much happening in her life. She had seemed to be all alone and just growing on her own.

"I feel a surge inside me too," Sammy thought. "I wonder if Angela's friends are also mine."

After the rain stopped, Sammy went to the briar patch that evening with mixed feelings.

What trust Angela had placed in him; yet some strange fears ran through his rabbit heart that made his tail stand still.

The next morning Sammy cut through the pumpkin patch to
see Angela. When he reached her she continued her tale.

"Sammy, I have told you about Mr. V, Mrs. S, Ms. DS, and you
have seen Ms. Rain. There is someone else, Ms. W. Her full
name is Ms. Gusty Wind. She is hard to see and comes from all
directions. Sometimes she comes from the north to cool me,
sometimes from the south to warm me, sometimes from the
west to scare me, and sometimes from the east to wake me. Ms. W
loves to play games and make my leaves dance. Someday I wish
I could fly away with her, fly as high as Harriet the Hawk.
I wonder what it would be like to be free from this patch. But
then I would miss you."

Sammy searched the sky to see Angela's invisible friend.

As he did so, he realized that the wind and rain, sun and soil, and
vine were also his friends. He decided to ask Angela a question.
"Does Ms. W ever tell any secrets?" Sammy asked. Angela
simply smiled and Sammy knew that Ms. W had many secrets.

The next day a very strange thing happened.

Halfway to the pumpkin patch, in between the sweet corn and the potatoes, Sammy's ears shot upright and he stood perfectly still. Then with utmost clarity he heard his name, "*Sammy, Sammy, Sammy.*" Three times it came and he knew the caller. It had to be Ms. W.

"How does Ms. W know my name?" Sammy wondered.

He stood as still as a mouse and listened carefully as Ms. W shared her secrets.

"Sammy," said Ms. W, "I have noticed your deep love for the beautiful Angela. Now I must share something with you. Mr. V and Mrs. S, Ms. DS and Ms. R, and I have a plan for all rabbits, cabbages, and pumpkins. Some day I will tell you about our plan for you, but today I want you to know about Angela.

"Farmer Jim works hard because all his brothers and sisters have needs, like your need for a carrot to keep your eyes from growing weak. Farmer Jim's family has a need for some beauty because their lives are hard and their hearts grow weary. That is why the pumpkins, especially one as lovely as Angela, are painted a beautiful orange. People need colors like your white tail against the green grass under a blue sky holding the yellow sun shining on the purple clover. Well, all these colors help Farmer Jim and his family to make it through the day.

"Now Sammy, I'm sorry but this will hurt your thumping heart so let me hold your paw. You see, all these people on the farm and in the city get hungry. Who will feed them? I've talked many hours with the members of the pumpkin patch and Angela has been one of the first volunteers. She is willing to become a pumpkin pie."

Sammy's heart stopped. His nose forgot to wiggle. His eyes grew weak and filled with tears. "Oh, no! Oh, no! Oh, no!" If Ms. W had not blown some breath Sammy's way to keep his heart beating, his nose wiggling, and his tears dry Sammy would have died on the spot.

Ms. W explained to Sammy how dying can lead to life. Sammy thought that knowing a secret took away the mystery. He was wrong. The mystery only got deeper.

"Sammy, not only will Angela feed people and make them happy, but she also volunteered a second time. She wants to be a lantern, too."

Sammy now knew how much Angela loved him.

You see, one night, Sammy, who always seemed so handsome and brave, opened his heart and told Angela his deepest secret.

He was afraid of the dark. He, brave Sammy, admitted it. He was afraid of the dark.

When Ms. W told Sammy about Angela's desire to become a lantern, he knew she did it just for him. The goblins would not scare Sammy this Halloween because Angela's smiling lantern would chase the goblins and darkness away. A big tear of love fell from Sammy's eye and made holy that place where he and Ms. W talked.

Poor Sammy! His thumping heart could hardly take in all of
this. But Ms. W had one more secret to share.

"Sammy, did you know that inside Angela there are seventy-five
seeds. Angela wants you, Sammy, to have all seventy-five seeds.
You are to have fifty to eat on the cold days of winter and
twenty-five seeds to plant next May. Angela wants to be with
you forever and ever and ever."

Sammy's heart and nose and tail were filled with sadness and
joy at the same time! All the way to the pumpkin patch he
smiled and cried, laughed and fell quiet, danced and hopped
along. It was a day he would always remember. He would never
be the same again.

In the distance, Farmer Jim saw Sammy and Angela talking together. He knew they had a special affection for one another. Farmer Jim loved Angela's bright orange smile. He loved Sammy's bushy tail. Now with a taste of autumn in the air, he wondered what the winter would bring. As long as the sun would shine, the wind would blow, and the rain would fall he had nothing to fear. It would be a good autumn.

It would be a good winter.

It would be a good spring.